THE CONRAN COOKBOOKS

ICED DELIGHTS

SHONA CRAWFORD POOLE

Doubleday & Company
Garden City, New York
1987

Photographs by Grant Symon

Conceived, designed and produced by
Conran Octopus Limited
28-32 Shelton Street
London WC2 9PH

First edition in United States

Title page: Strawberry Ice Cream Cake (page 66)

Library of Congress Cataloging-in-Publication Data

Poole, Shona Crawford.
  Iced delights.

  (Conran cookbooks)
  1. Ice cream, ices, etc.   2. Desserts, Frozen.
I. Title.   II. Series.
TX795.P66   1987   641.8'62   86-16547
ISBN 0-385-23814-2

Printed in Spain

CONTENTS

INTRODUCTION

Real ices made with ripe fruit, fresh cream and natural flavors are a startling improvement on what most mass manufacturers call ice cream. The stuff they make with all those nameless fats, unpronounceable emulsifiers, numbered flavorings and coded colors is edible, but it is not the stuff of frozen dreams.

The chefs who run the finest restaurants make sorbets daily. The reason is not that they cannot make sufficient at once to last for a week or two, but because ices taste best fresh. For many cooks this is a counsel of perfection that will take second place to the convenience of having iced desserts on tap. But it is worth noticing the difference freshness makes.

Freezing in an ice cream machine

If they have not already succumbed to ownership of an electric ice cream machine which freezes and churns simultaneously, serious ice cream lovers will be weighing up the cost against storage space and high-quality results.

It has to be said that ices made in the big ice cream machines, or in the old fashioned hand-cranked churns, do have the smoothest, finest texture. This is due to the constant beating, of course, but also to the high speed at which they freeze – usually less than half an hour.

Electric freezer churns, the newest type of ice cream machine designed for domestic use, are the most expensive. They are also the bulkiest machines, about the size of a heavy-duty typewriter, and quite a weight to lift. Against that, they make smooth ices quickly and efficiently. Models with a freezer bowl that can be removed for washing have an obvious advantage.

Hand-cranked churns requiring the addition of ice, salt and human motor-power make ices as smooth as those produced in electric freezer churns. And although they cost less than the newer models, they are not cheap.

Small electric ice cream machines that churn the mixture inside your freezer – the rubber door seals accommodate the cord – are the least costly ice cream makers. In my experience the texture of the ices is not as smooth as that of ices made in the larger machines, nor is it a significant improvement on still-frozen ices. But if the convenience of forgetting the mixture once it is in the freezer counts, then one of these machines is worth considering. Best are models with paddles which automatically lift clear of the ice before it freezes hard.

Still-freezing

Still-freezing, as the term suggests, means freezing without simultaneously stirring. It simply involves using an ordinary container for the ice cream mixture and putting it in the freezer until it is firm. Most ice creams and sorbets need whisking or beating vigorously during the freezing process to break up the ice crystals, making the ice pleasantly smooth.

As a general rule, the richer or sweeter the recipe the less stirring or whisking it will need. Large flakes or crystals of ice form most readily in the least sweet or creamy ices, which must be taken out of the freezer and beaten to reduce the size of the ice crystals, at least once or twice during the freezing process.

The best possible time to beat any ice that does require whisking while it freezes is when the sides and bottom are almost firm and the center is fairly liquid. The ice should be tipped into a chilled bowl and beaten really vigorously. This can also be done in a food processor, but it does not achieve quite the same aerating effect as a well-timed beating. The whisked ice is then returned to the freezer to firm again. An overlooked ice that has frozen hard before beating is better softened in the refrigerator than at room temperature.

There are also plenty of ices in this book which can be frozen without any stirring at all, using any kind of freezer. Most of these are simple to make too, and most of them are either fairly sweet, or rich — or both — because sugar and fat are two ingredients which, like alcohol, inhibit the formation of large, gritty ice crystals. Another is gelatin, but its uses are limited in ice cream making.

When still-freezing, always turn the freezer to its coldest setting for at least an hour beforehand. The colder the temperature, the smaller the crystals of ice formed in the mixture. For the same reason, it helps to freeze ices in flat containers which are in direct contact with the freezing element. (Only the sorbets containing alcohol require a 0°F freezer or a freezer churn.)

Freezing times

Freezing times are so variable that even the vaguest instructions can be more misleading than helpful. One reason is that the relatively inefficient ice-making compartment of a small refrigerator will take much longer to do the job than a modern freezer working on its fast-freeze setting.

Containers affect freezing times too. Metal is a better conductor of cold than plastic, and a shallow metal tray in contact with the freezer element is the most efficient way to freeze any ice quickly.

The type of ingredients used also affects freezing times. Recipes with a high proportion of sugar or alcohol will generally take longest to freeze.

When still-freezing it may be wise to avoid the possible disappointment of half frozen ices by making them the day before they are needed.

Ripening

After a day or two in the freezer, most ices will be rock-hard and will require 'ripening' to show themselves at their best. Ripening or softening an ice to the consistency which makes the most of its flavor and texture should always be done slowly in the refrigerator — never hurried in a warm kitchen. The aim is to soften it enough to scoop and serve, or to eat and, as with freezing, timing will depend on the same factors.

Small quantities, individual servings or ices in flat containers will ripen more quickly than ices in deep containers or bombes. Small ices will need only 5 or 10 minutes. Bombes or big containers up to 30 minutes.

The sweetest and most alcoholic ices will tend to ripen fastest, and those from the most efficient freezers will take longer to ripen than those made in less cold ice-making compartments of small refrigerators.

Shona Crawford Poole

RHUBARB SORBET

Forced spring rhubarb first appears in the depths of winter and makes and unusual pale pink ice. The flavor is perfectly captured by baking the rhubarb with sugar and no added liquid.

——————— SERVES 6 ———————

1¼ lb spring rhubarb
1¼ cups sugar

Heat the oven to 350°F.

Chop the rhubarb into short lengths and put it into a deep ovenproof dish with the sugar. Cover closely and bake for 45 minutes or until the rhubarb is very tender. Set it aside to cool.

Blend or process the fruit with its juice, or press it through a fine sieve to make a smooth purée.

Freeze in an ice cream machine following the manufacturer's instructions. Or still-freeze (page 4), vigorously whisking the partially frozen ice at least once during the freezing process.

APPLE AND HONEY SORBET

This smooth apple sorbet is peachy-pink and intensely flavored. Beware of overpowering the apple taste with a too highly scented honey. A hint of honey is lovely. Choose apples of character — whether eaters or cookers. Newton Pippins and Winesaps are good.

——————— SERVES 6 ———————

5 cups unsweetened apple juice
1½ lb apples
¾ cup sugar
2 tablespoons clear honey

Put the apple juice into a heavy saucepan, bring to a boil and simmer, uncovered, until reduced to about 2½ cups.

Peel, core and roughly chop the apples. Add the apples and sugar to the juice and cook gently until the apples are tender. Stir in the honey and set aside to cool.

Blend or process the apples to a smooth purée, or pass through a fine sieve.

Freeze in an ice cream machine following the manufacturer's instructions. Or still-freeze (page 4), vigorously whisking the partially frozen ice at least once during the freezing process.

Left: Apple and Honey Sorbet, right: Rhubarb Sorbet.

Top: Seville Orange Sorbet, below: Pink Grapefruit and Mint Sorbet, left: Lime and Green Ginger Sorbet (page 10).

SEVILLE ORANGE SORBET

Capture the inimitable flavor of marmalade oranges during their brief new year season in this distinctive bitter orange sorbet. The ice is lightened with egg white, a technique which works best with strong flavors. Use the same recipe for the other sour citrus fruits — limes, lemons and grapefruit.
Because their peel is invariably eaten, Seville oranges are not treated with fungicidal wax. This means that they do not keep as well as treated citrus fruits and should be used as soon as possible.

─────── SERVES 6 ───────

1 lb Seville oranges
1 cup granulated sugar
1⅞ cups water
2 egg whites

Cut the peel from the oranges, using a very sharp knife, taking only a thin layer of rind and none of the pith.

Put the rind into a saucepan with the sugar and water and heat gently until the sugar has dissolved completely. Raise the heat and boil the syrup for 5 minutes, then set it aside to cool completely.

Squeeze the juice from the oranges and strain it. Strain the cooled syrup, then stir it into the orange juice.

To freeze in an ice cream machine: lightly whisk the egg whites, combine them with the syrup, then freeze immediately, following the manufacturer's instructions.

To still-freeze (page 4): freeze the syrup to a heavy slush, then whisk the egg whites until they are stiff and beat them lightly into the partially frozen mixture. Freeze until the ice is a little firmer, then vigorously whisk once more for a really smooth sorbet. Return it to the freezer until it is firm.

PINK GRAPEFRUIT AND MINT SORBET

This is tart, refreshing and not too sweet. It could be served as a first course on a hot summer day.

─────── SERVES 6 ───────

3 large pink grapefruit
¾ cup sugar
1¼ cups water
4 tablespoons chopped fresh mint

Cut the peel from one of the grapefruit, using a very sharp knife, taking only a thin layer of rind and none of the pith.

Put the rind into a saucepan with the sugar and water and heat gently until the sugar has dissolved completely. Simmer the syrup for 5 minutes, then take it off the heat and stir in the mint. Set it aside until quite cold.

Squeeze the juice from all the grapefruit and strain it. Strain the cold syrup and stir it into the grapefruit juice.

Freeze in an ice cream machine following the manufacturer's instructions. Or still-freeze (page 4), vigorously whisking the partially frozen ice at least once during the freezing process.

More chopped mint can be stirred into the partially frozen sorbet for a pretty, mintier effect.

LIME AND GREEN GINGER SORBET

Illustrated on page 8

Experiment to discover how much ginger you like in this tantalizingly hot and cold ice.

SERVES 6
---

4 limes
1½-in cube fresh ginger root, sliced
1 cup granulated sugar
1⅞ cup water
2 egg whites

Cut the peel from one of the limes, using a very sharp knife, taking only the rind and none of the pith.

Put the rind into a saucepan with the ginger, sugar and water. Heat gently until the sugar has dissolved completely, then simmer the syrup for 5 minutes. Set it aside for at least 12 hours to cool completely and infuse with the flavor of the ginger.

Squeeze the juice from all the limes and strain it. Strain the syrup, then stir it into the lime juice.

To freeze in an ice cream machine: lightly whisk the egg whites, combine them with the syrup, then freeze immediately, following the manufacturer's instructions.

To still-freeze (page 4): freeze the syrup to a heavy slush, then whisk the egg whites until they are stiff and beat them lightly into the partially frozen mixture. Freeze until the ice is a little firmer, then vigorously whisk once more for a really smooth sorbet. Return it to the freezer until it is firm.

ICED PEARS

Fresh pears for filling should be shapely and slightly under-ripe. A potato peeler is a good tool for beginning to hollow out fruit and a teaspoon finishes the job neatly.

SERVES 6
---

8 large, not too ripe pears
6 tablespoons fresh lemon juice
1½ cups sugar
2⅛ cups water

Cut the tops off all the pears, removing a lid of flesh with the stalk. Drop the lids into a large bowl of cold water acidulated with 1 tablespoon of the lemon juice to prevent the pears from discoloring. Hollow out the pears, leaving a shell about ¼ in thick. Put them into the acidulated water as soon as they are ready. Reserve the scooped-out flesh and cores.

Put the sugar and water into a large saucepan and heat gently until the sugar has dissolved completely. Raise the heat and boil the syrup for 2 minutes, then add the hollowed pears and the lids and bring the syrup back to a boil. Simmer for a further 2 minutes, then carefully remove the pears and lids from the syrup and drain on paper towel.

Choose the 6 best pears and lids and set them aside to cool. When they are quite cold set them on a sheet of baking parchment, leveling the bases if necessary to make them stand upright. Freeze them hard.

In the meantime, chop the 2 remaining hollowed pears and cook with the reserved pear flesh in the syrup until tender. Pass the fruit with the syrup through a fine sieve to make a smooth purée. Stir in the remaining lemon juice and leave to cool.

Freeze in an ice cream machine following the manufacturer's instructions. Or still-freeze (page 4), vigorously whisking the mixture at least twice during the freezing process. While the ice is still soft enough to stir, use it to fill the prepared pear cases. Top with the lids and freeze again until firm.

Above: Iced Pears.

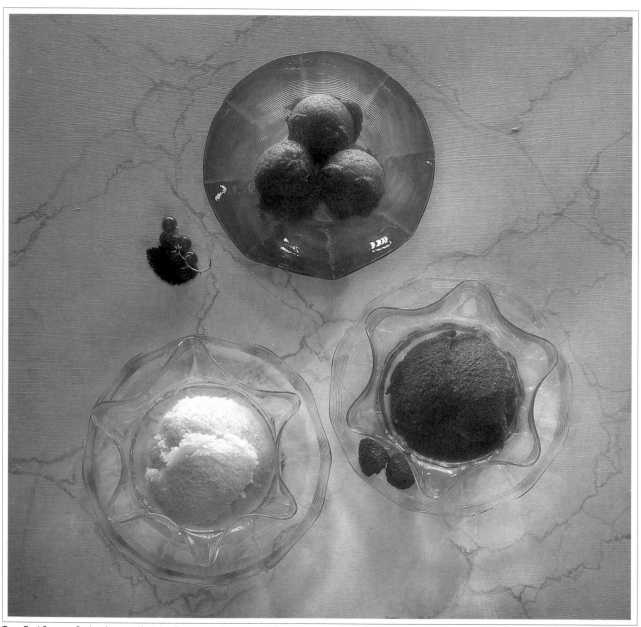

Top: Red Currant Sorbet (page 16), right: Raspberry Sorbet, left: Gooseberry and Elderberry Sorbet.

RASPBERRY SORBET

Raspberries need no cooking to turn them into fresh-tasting sorbets. Both fresh and frozen berries are suitable for ices. This recipe can be used for a variety of other intensely flavored soft fruits, including ripe strawberries, loganberries and mangoes.

—————— SERVES 6 ——————

1 lb ripe raspberries, thawed if frozen
1½ cups Basic Sorbet Syrup (page 78)
juice of 1 orange, strained

Rub the raspberries through a fine sieve to remove the seeds, or process them briefly in a blender or food processor and strain the purée. Combine the purée with the syrup and orange juice. If you have time, chill the purée for 1-2 hours in the refrigerator before freezing it. This step allows the flavor to develop.

Freeze in an ice cream machine following the manufacturer's instructions. Or still-freeze (page 4), vigorously whisking the partially frozen ice at least once during the freezing process.

GOOSEBERRY AND ELDERFLOWER SORBET

Even town rats can find elderflowers in municipal parks and cascading over the gas works wall in early summer when the first green gooseberries appear. Together they make a sorbet exotically perfumed like muscat grapes.

—————— SERVES 6 ——————

2 lb green gooseberries
1 pint water
1 cup granulated sugar
about 3 large elderflower heads

Wash the gooseberries (there is no need to cut off their ends) and put them, whole, into a saucepan with the water. Simmer the fruit until it is tender, then strain the juice through a scalded jelly bag, or through a large sieve lined with a clean cloth. Knot the corners of the cloth and hang it until it stops dripping.

Tie the elderflower heads loosely in a piece of muslin and put them into a saucepan with the gooseberry juice and the sugar. Heat gently until the sugar has dissolved completely, bring to a boil, then cool immediately. By the time the syrup is quite cold, the elderflowers will have perfumed it strongly.

Discard the elderflowers and freeze the syrup in an ice cream machine following the manufacturer's instructions. Or still-freeze (page 4), vigorously whisking the partially frozen mixture twice during the freezing process.

CARAMEL SORBET

This must be the simplest sorbet of all — just sugar, water and a dash of lemon juice.

──────── SERVES 6 ────────

1½ cups sugar
3 cups water
juice of 1 lemon

Put the sugar and ⅔ cup of the water into a heavy saucepan and heat gently until the sugar has dissolved completely. Wash down any sugar crystals from the sides of the pan with a pastry brush dipped in cold water.

Raise the heat and boil the syrup to a light caramel, no darker than a rich golden brown or the sorbet will be bitter instead of sweet. Immediately remove the saucepan from the heat and dip its base into cold water to stop the sugar from darkening still further.

Add the remaining water to the caramel and leave it to dissolve and cool, stirring from time to time to hasten the process.

When the syrup is quite cold, stir in the lemon juice.

Freeze in an ice cream machine following the manufacturer's instructions. Or still-freeze (page 4), vigorously whisking the partially frozen ice at least once during the freezing process. The more frequently it is beaten during freezing the smoother the sorbet will be.

CHOCOLATE SORBET

Because it has so much less fat than chocolate, cocoa is better for making this smooth, chocolate-flavored sorbet.

──────── SERVES 6 ────────

1½ cups sugar
2⅛ cups water
vanilla extract
½ cup cocoa

Put the sugar and water into a saucepan and heat gently until the sugar has dissolved completely. Raise the heat and boil the syrup for 1 minute, then remove from the heat and allow it to cool a little.

Stir a little of the syrup into the cocoa in a bowl, to make a smooth paste, then gradually stir in the remaining syrup.

Add vanilla extract to taste, remembering that the flavor of the finished ice will be dulled by freezing. Strain the mixture.

Freeze in an ice cream machine following the manufacturer's instructions. Or still-freeze (page 4), vigorously whisking the partially frozen ice at least once during the freezing process.

Left: Chocolate Sorbet, right: Caramel Sorbet.

RED CURRANT SORBET

Illustrated on page 12

The flavor of soft fruits like red currants and black currants is enhanced by gently heating the fruit to extract the juice.

———————— SERVES 6 ————————

1½ lb red currants
1 cup sugar

Heat the oven to 350°F.

Wash the red currants (there is no need to cut off the ends) and shake off the excess water. Put them into a deep ovenproof dish with the sugar. Cover closely and bake for 30-45 minutes, or until the juices have run and the fruit is tender.

Pass the cooked red currants through a fine sieve to remove the skins, seeds and stalks. Leave the juice to cool completely.

Freeze in an ice cream machine following the manufacturer's instructions. Or still-freeze (page 4), vigorously whisking the partially frozen ice at least once during the freezing process.

CLARET GRANITA

Granitas are intentionally crunchy ices. An occasional, desultory stir — and no beating — during freezing is all that is required to produce the flaky crystals of ice that are their hallmark. Raspberries have an affinity with red wine which is shown to advantage in this ice.

———————— SERVES 6 ————————

4 oz (¼ lb) fresh or frozen raspberries, thawed if frozen
¾ cup sugar
½ cup water
1 bottle red Bordeaux wine

Mash the raspberries or process in a blender or food processor, then pass the pulp through a fine sieve to remove the seeds. Set the purée aside.

Put the sugar and water into a small saucepan and heat gently until the sugar has dissolved completely. Raise the heat and boil the syrup for 5 minutes, then set it aside to cool.

When the syrup is quite cold, combine it with the raspberry purée and the wine.

To still-freeze: pour the mixture into a shallow, flat-bottomed container (preferably a metal tray, but a plastic box will also do) and freeze until the edges are firm and the center of the ice is still liquid. Stir the sides to the center with a fork, then return the mixture to the freezer until firm.

The same recipe frozen in an ice cream machine to make a smooth ice is also delightful.

Above: Claret Granita.

Left: Champagne Sorbet, right: Sorbet de Beaumes de Venise.

CHAMPAGNE SORBET

Like champagne cocktails, champagne ices call for nothing too grand in the way of wine and rely on other ingredients for much of their flavor. Alcohol inhibits the formation of ice crystals, so this ice never freezes really hard at domestic freezer temperatures and needs no ripening before serving.

———— SERVES 6 ————

2 juicy oranges
½ cup sugar
½ cup water
2½ cups non-vintage champagne
4 tablespoons brandy
¼ teaspoon angostura or orange bitters

Cut the peel from the oranges, using a very sharp knife, taking only the rind and none of the pith. Squeeze, strain and reserve the juice.

Put the orange rind, sugar and water into a saucepan and heat gently until the sugar has dissolved completely. Raise the heat and boil the syrup for 5 minutes, then set it aside to cool.

When the syrup is cold, discard the orange rind and stir the orange juice, champagne, brandy and bitters into the cold syrup.

Freeze in an ice cream machine following the manufacturer's instructions. Or still-freeze (page 4), vigorously whisking the partially frozen ice at least once during the freezing process.

SORBET DE BEAUMES-DE-VENISE

After years in the wilderness, dessert wines came back into fashion with Muscat de Beaumes-de-Venise. With its rich taste of muscat grapes, it is robust enough to make an excellent ice with little in the way of other additions. This is also true of many Barsacs, Tokays and other sweet wines.

———— SERVES 6 ————

½ cup sugar
½ cup water
juice of 1 lemon
2½ cups Muscat de Beaumes-de-Venise
1 egg white

Put the sugar and water into a small saucepan and heat gently until the sugar has dissolved completely. Raise the heat and boil the syrup for 5 minutes, then set it aside to cool. Stir in the lemon juice and wine.

To freeze in an ice cream machine: lightly whisk the egg white, combine it with the syrup, then freeze immediately, following the manufacturer's instructions.

To still-freeze (page 4): freeze the syrup to a heavy slush, then whisk the egg whites until they are stiff and beat them lightly into the partially frozen mixture. Freeze until the ice is a little firmer, then vigorously whisk once more for a really smooth sorbet. Return it to the freezer until it is firm.

APPLE AND CALVADOS SORBET

Fresh fruit juice fortified with a liqueur of the same flavor makes a quick and elegant sorbet. Basic Sorbet Syrup speeds the process still further. Alternatively, make a syrup with ½ cup sugar and ¾ cup water. This ice will probably not require ripening, and can be served straight from the freezer.

——— SERVES 6 ———

1⅞ cups unsweetened apple juice
1¼ cups Basic Sorbet Syrup (page 78)
4 tablespoons fresh lemon juice
4 tablespoons calvados

Combine the apple juice with the sorbet syrup, lemon juice and calvados.

Freeze in an ice cream machine following the manufacturer's instructions. Or still-freeze (page 4), vigorously whisking the partially frozen ice at least once during the freezing process.

PORT SLUSH

Port needs no additional sugar to make a superbly luxurious and alcoholic ice. This is a dense ice but does not freeze hard, so may be served straight from the freezer without ripening.

——— SERVES 6 ———

1¼ cups fresh orange juice
1⅞ cups port

Strain the orange juice and combine it with the port.

Freeze in an ice cream machine following the manufacturer's instructions. Or still-freeze (page 4), vigorously whisking the partially frozen ice at least once during the freezing process.

Left: Apple and Calvados Sorbet, right: Port Slush.

Top: Jaeger Tea Sorbet, below: Poire William Sorbet.

POIRE WILLIAM SORBET

All manner of fruits flavor the strong, colorless spirits which are especially popular in the mountainous regions of Europe. The pear and raspberry-flavored varieties are the most successful in sorbets.

─────────── SERVES 6 ───────────

1 cup sugar
1½ cups water
6 tablespoons Poire William eau-de-vie
2 tablespoons fresh lemon juice
1 egg white

Put the sugar and water into a saucepan and heat gently until the sugar has dissolved completely. Raise the heat and boil the syrup for 5 minutes. Set it aside to cool. When the syrup is quite cold, stir in the Poire William eau-de-vie and lemon juice.

To freeze in an ice cream machine: lightly whisk the egg white, combine it with the syrup, then freeze immediately, following the manufacturer's instructions.

To still-freeze (page 4): freeze the syrup to a heavy slush, then whisk the egg white until it is stiff and beat it lightly into the partially frozen mixture. Freeze until the ice is a little firmer, then vigorously whisk once more for a really smooth sorbet. Return it to the freezer.

JAEGER TEA SORBET

Jaeger tea — hot tea with rum — is Austria's version of the hot toddy. No doubt the Jaegers, or hunters, welcomed its cheer more warmly than a set of the good Dr Jaeger's long woolly underwear. To extract the maximum flavor and minimum tannin from any tea, use the following formula to calculate the optimum brewing time. Put the leaves into a heated container and pour freshly boiled water over them. The leaves will rise to the surface like the head on a glass of beer. Time how long they take to sink and you have that tea's ideal brewing time. Adjust the strength by altering the quantity of tea leaves. Indian or Ceylon tea is ideal for this sorbet.

─────────── SERVES 6 ───────────

1 lemon
3¾ cups strong black tea
½ cup sugar or packed brown sugar
6 tablespoons rum

Cut the peel from the lemon, using a very sharp knife, taking only a thin layer of rind and none of the pith. Squeeze the juice and set it aside.

Put the tea into a saucepan with the sugar and lemon rind. Heat gently until the sugar has dissolved completely. Set it aside to cool completely, then discard the rind and stir in the rum.

Taste the syrup and add a little lemon juice to taste.

Freeze in an ice cream machine following the manufacturer's instructions. Or still-freeze (page 4), vigorously whisking the partially frozen ice at least once during the freezing process.

VANILLA ICE CREAM

Real, old-fashioned vanilla ice cream made with an egg custard is the basis of many more perennial favorites. To transform it into cassata ice cream, stir a mixture of chopped dried and candied fruit into vanilla ice cream which has been frozen but is not yet quite firm. To make chocolate chip, grate hard chocolate, milk or plain, and stir it into the partially frozen ice. For rum and raisin, add raisins which have been soaked overnight in rum, or in a rum-flavored syrup.

The recipe which follows is for a classic vanilla ice cream. Of course the quantity of sugar may be reduced by as much as half, and skimmed or semi-skimmed milk substituted for whole milk. The result will obviously be less rich and less sweet. It will also be a little crisper. Egg custards thicken below the boiling point, and must not boil or they will curdle. It is a good idea to use a double boiler, or a bowl over simmering water.

———— SERVES 6 ————

1 vanilla pod or real vanilla extract
2⅛ cups milk
6 egg yolks
1¼ cups sugar
a pinch of salt

If using a vanilla pod, halve it lengthways and put it into a heavy saucepan with the milk. Heat gently to near boiling point, then remove from the heat and set it aside for 30 minutes. If using vanilla extract, there is no need to heat the milk. Add vanilla extract to taste once the custard has cooled.

Combine the egg yolks, sugar and salt in a bowl. Whisk until the mixture is very pale and falls back leaving a trail when the beaters are lifted. Strain the milk and gradually whisk it in. Return the mixture to the pan and cook it over a very low heat, or cook it in the top of a double boiler, stirring constantly until the custard is thick enough to coat the back of a wooden spoon.

Remove the custard from the heat and set it aside to cool, stirring it from time to time to prevent a skin forming. Vanilla extract should be added at this point, remembering that the flavor will fade with freezing.

Freeze in an ice cream machine following the manufacturer's instructions. Or still-freeze (page 4), vigorously whisking the partially frozen ice at least once during the freezing process.

BUTTERSCOTCH ICE CREAM

Butter and brown sugar cooked together until the sugar caramelizes give a rich butterscotch flavor to this unusual ice.

———— SERVES 6 ————

6 tablespoons (¾ stick) butter
1 cup packed brown sugar
2⅛ cups hot milk
4 egg yolks, beaten

Melt the butter in a heavy saucepan and stir in the sugar. Cook the mixture slowly until the sugar begins to caramelize, watching it very carefully so that it does not become too dark. Remove from the heat and stir in the hot milk, and continue stirring until the toffee has dissolved completely.

Allow the flavored milk to cool a little, then gradually stir it into the egg yolks in a bowl. Strain the mixture back into the pan and cook it carefully over a low heat, or cook it in the top of a double boiler, stirring constantly until the custard is thick enough to coat the back of a wooden spoon.

Remove the custard from the heat and set it aside to cool, stirring it from time to time to prevent a skin forming.

Freeze in an ice cream machine following the manufacturer's instructions. Or still-freeze (page 4), vigorously whisking the partially frozen ice at least once during the freezing process.

Left: Chocolate Chip Ice Cream, center: Butterscotch Ice Cream, right: Vanilla Ice Cream.

Left: Hazelnut Ice Cream, right: Praline Ice Cream with biscuit cigars.

PRALINE ICE CREAM

Toasted nuts and brittle caramel ground together to a fine powder are an indispensable flavoring in confectionery, pâtisserie and ices. Almonds and hazels are the best nuts for praline.

─────── **SERVES 6** ───────

4 egg yolks
1 cup sugar
1⅞ cup milk
1½ cups blanched almonds
⅔ cup whipping cream

Heat the oven to 325°F.

Combine the egg yolks with 6 oz of the sugar in a bowl. Whisk until the mixture is very pale and falls back leaving a trail when the beaters are lifted. Gradually whisk in the milk.

Cook the custard carefully in a heavy saucepan over a low heat, or cook it in the top of a double boiler, stirring constantly until it is thick enough to coat the back of a wooden spoon. Take the custard off the heat and cool, stirring it from time to time to prevent a skin forming.

Meanwhile, spread the almonds on a baking sheet and toast them in the oven for about 10 minutes or until they are lightly browned. Then spread the almonds on a lightly oiled surface.

Put the remaining sugar and 4 tablespoons of water into a small, heavy saucepan and heat gently until it has dissolved and turns a deep golden brown. Immediately pour the caramel over the nuts – it does not matter if it does not cover all of them – and leave until cold. Then crush the praline to a fine powder in an electric coffee grinder or with a pestle and mortar.

Stir the praline into the cold custard. Whip the cream until it holds soft peaks and fold it in.

Freeze in an ice cream machine following the manufacturer's instructions. Or still-freeze (page 4), vigorously whisking the partially frozen ice at least once during the freezing process.

HAZELNUT ICE CREAM

Nut ices are seldom available commercially and yet they are among the most appealing. Hazels, almonds, walnuts and pistachios all make excellent ice creams. Use the Vanilla Ice Cream custard base (page 24), omitting the vanilla flavoring, or try this richer recipe. Like hazelnuts, almonds are best toasted before grinding. Walnuts and pistachios need no cooking, but add a couple of tablespoons of sweet sherry to the walnut variation, and a few drops of almond essence to the custard for pistachio ice cream.

─────── **SERVES 6** ───────

1 cup shelled hazelnuts
4 egg yolks
¾ cup sugar
1¼ cups milk
⅔ cups whipping cream

Heat the oven to 325°F.

Spread the hazelnuts on a baking sheet and toast them in the oven for 10-15 minutes, or until their centers are a pale biscuit color. Turn the nuts on to a cloth and rub off the skins. Cool, then process them in a food processor or electric coffee mill. Set aside.

Combine the egg yolks and sugar in a bowl. Whisk until the mixture is very pale and falls back leaving a trail when the beaters are lifted. Gradually beat in the milk. Cook the custard carefully in a heavy saucepan over a low heat, or cook it in the top of a double boiler, stirring constantly until it is thick enough to coat the back of a wooden spoon. Take the custard off the heat and set it aside to cool, stirring it from time to time to prevent a skin forming.

Stir the ground hazelnuts into the cold custard. Whip the cream until it holds soft peaks and fold it in.

Freeze in an ice cream machine following the manufacturer's instructions. Or still-freeze (page 4), vigorously whisking the partially frozen ice at least once during the freezing process.

CARDAMOM AND PISTACHIO ICE CREAM

The flavorings of this ice are Indian, but its creamy texture is decidedly European. Cardamom is an expensive spice, but only a little is needed in any one recipe. Scandinavians use it extensively in their baking and can buy ground cardamom with ease. When using the whole spice, remove the aromatic seeds from their surrounding pods and crush them with a little sugar with a pestle and mortar. For a real Indian touch, decorate each serving with edible silver leaf, found in Indian shops. This is real silver beaten out as thinly as tissue paper.

SERVES 6

½ cup sugar
½ cup water
1⅞ cups evaporated milk
about ¼ teaspoon ground cardamom
½ cup shelled pistachio nuts, chopped
⅔ cup whipping cream

Put the sugar and water into a heavy saucepan and heat gently until the sugar has dissolved completely. Raise the heat and boil the syrup for 5 minutes. Set it aside to cool, then stir in the evaporated milk, cardamom, pistachio nuts and lightly whipped cream.

Freeze in an ice cream machine following the manufacturer's instructions. Or still-freeze (page 4), vigorously whisking the partially frozen ice at least once during the freezing process.

SAFFRON AND MACE ICE CREAM

A few strands of saffron are enough to perfume a whole batch of ice cream with the spice's earthy warmth and to color it bright yellow. Mace, another warm spice, should be freshly ground if it is to be at its best. If mace is not available, use freshly grated nutmeg.

SERVES 6

¼ teaspoon saffron strands
2⅛ cups milk
6 egg yolks
1¼ cups sugar
1 teaspoon ground mace

Put the saffron into a ladle and heat it over a naked flame to encourage it to release its color and perfume. Take care that it does not darken too much or burn.

Put the milk and saffron into a large saucepan. Bring almost to a boil, then remove from the heat and leave to infuse for 30 minutes.

Combine the egg yolks and sugar in a bowl. Whisk until the mixture is very pale and falls back leaving a trail when the beaters are lifted. Strain the milk and gradually whisk it into the egg mixture.

Cook the custard carefully in a heavy saucepan over a low heat, or cook it in the top of a double boiler, stirring constantly until it is thick enough to coat the back of a wooden spoon. Remove the custard from the heat, stir in the mace and set it aside to cool, stirring it from time to time to prevent a skin forming.

Freeze in an ice cream machine following the manufacturer's instructions. Or still-freeze (page 4), vigorously whisking the partially frozen ice at least once during the freezing process.

Left: Saffron and Mace Ice Cream, right: Cardamom and Pistachio Ice Cream with Tuiles (page 72).

Left: Chocolate Ice Cream, center: Butterfly Shortcake Thins (page 73), top: Coffee Ice Cream in Meringue Nest (page 76).

COFFEE ICE CREAM

Freshly roasted and ground coffee, especially if it is a high or dark roast, makes a superb flavoring for ices. Instant coffee can be used instead, of course, but the ice will have less distinction.

----------- SERVES 6 -----------

¾ cup boiling water
4 tablespoons finely ground fresh coffee
6 egg yolks
1 cup packed brown sugar
2½ cups milk

Use the water and coffee to make fresh filter coffee, or pour the water onto the coffee, infuse for a few minutes, then strain.

Combine the egg yolks and sugar in a bowl. Whisk until the mixture is very pale and falls back leaving a trail when the beaters are lifted. Whisk in the coffee and milk.

Cook the custard carefully in a heavy saucepan over a low heat, or cook it in the top of a double boiler, stirring constantly until it is thick enough to coat the back of a wooden spoon.

Take the custard off the heat, and set it aside to cool, stirring it from time to time to prevent a skin forming.

Freeze in an ice cream machine following the manufacturer's instructions. Or still-freeze (page 4), vigorously whisking the partially frozen ice at least once during the freezing process.

CHOCOLATE ICE CREAM

This recipe uses good dark chocolate and avoids an over-sweet or over-rich mixture which would mask the chocolate flavor. Numerous variations on the basic formula are successful. To add a true orange flavor rub the skin of an orange with a half dozen sugar cubes and dissolve them in the hot custard. Or combine the partially frozen ice with flaked almonds which have been toasted lightly and cooled.

----------- SERVES 6 -----------

6 egg yolks
½ cup sugar
1¼ cups milk
1¼ cups light cream
8 oz (½ lb) good-quality dark chocolate, grated
real vanilla extract

Combine the egg yolks and sugar in a bowl. Whisk until the mixture is very pale and falls back in a trail when the beaters are lifted. Whisk in the milk, followed by the cream.

Cook the custard carefully in a heavy saucepan over a low heat, or cook it in the top of a double boiler, stirring constantly until it is thick enough to coat the back of a wooden spoon. Remove it from the heat.

Stir the chocolate into the hot custard, then add a few drops of vanilla extract. Leave the custard to cool, stirring it from time to time to prevent a skin forming.

Freeze in an ice cream machine following the manufacturer's instructions. Or still-freeze (page 4), vigorously whisking the partially frozen ice at least once during the freezing process.

LECHE MERENGADA

*Spanish cinnamon ices are classics of another kind —
crisp milk ices lightened with egg whites. This recipe is
adapted from one given in* The Foods and Wines of
Spain *by Penelope Casas (Penguin Books, 1985).*

──────── SERVES 6 ────────

1 lemon
2½ cups milk
1 cup heavy cream
¾ cup sugar
2 × 4-in cinnamon sticks
2 egg whites
ground cinnamon

Cut the peel from the lemon, using a very sharp knife,
taking only the rind and none of the pith. Squeeze the
lemon and reserve the juice.

Put the lemon rind into a heavy saucepan with the
milk, cream, sugar and cinnamon sticks and heat gently,
stirring until the sugar has dissolved completely. Then
raise the heat and simmer the mixture for about 30
minutes. Set it aside to cool completely, then discard
the lemon rind and cinnamon sticks.

Whisk the egg whites with a teaspoon of the lemon
juice until they hold soft peaks. Beat in the flavored milk.

Freeze in an ice cream machine following the manufacturer's instructions. Or still-freeze (page 4), vigorously whisking the partially frozen ice at least once during
the freezing process. Dust each serving with a little
ground cinnamon.

BROWN BREAD ICE CREAM

*Ices made with toasted brown bread crumbs have been
popular in England since the latter half of the eighteenth
century. The Victorians decorated this ice with
crystalized violets (page 78). Fresh raspberries are good
too. Use robust whole-wheat bread for this recipe.*

──────── SERVES 6 ────────

1½ cups whole-wheat bread crumbs
⅜ cup sugar
4 tablespoons water
1⅞ cups heavy cream
1½ cup confectioner's sugar, sifted
2 tablespoons rum
real vanilla extract

Spread the crumbs on a baking tray and toast under a
grill or broiler, stirring from time to time, until an even
golden brown. Be careful not to burn them. Set aside to
cool.

Put the sugar and water into a saucepan and heat
gently until the sugar has dissolved completely. Wash
down any crystals from the sides of the pan with a
pastry brush dipped in cold water. Raise the heat and
boil the syrup to a rich brown caramel. Do not allow the
caramel to darken too much or it will be bitter. Take it off
the heat and stir in the crumbs.

Immediately turn the mixture onto a buttered baking
tray. It will harden quickly to a kind of poor man's
praline. Grind it finely in a coffee grinder or with a pestle
and mortar. Do not try to grind this very hard mixture in a
food processor or blender. It may damage the blades.
Whip the cream until it holds soft peaks, then beat in the
icing sugar, rum and a little vanilla extract. Fold in the
sugared crumbs and still-freeze (page 4) without stirring.

Top; Brown Bread Ice Cream, below: Leche Merengada in Tuile Basket (page 72).

Left: Honey Ice Cream with Lavender (page 36), center: Rich Vanilla Ice Cream (page 36) in Brandy Snap Basket (page 73), right: Lemon Ice Cream.

LEMON ICE CREAM

Smooth, creamy ices that can be frozen without stirring are quick and easy to make, but they do tend to be rich. It is the quantity of cream that makes these mixtures freeze successfully without requiring constant beating to reduce the size of the ice crystals.
This lemon ice cream is quite simply sumptuous, as are Seville orange or lime ice creams made in the same manner. It may be frozen in individual serving containers — hollowed out lemons are most attractive. It can also be used as a piped topping for more elaborate frozen desserts.

SERVES 6
---

3 juicy lemons
1½ cups confectioner's sugar
1⅞ cups heavy cream
3 tablespoons iced water

Using the finest blade on the grater, grate the rind from 2 of the lemons, and squeeze the juice from all 3. Combine the rind, juice and sugar and if possible set aside for 30 minutes to allow the flavor to develop.

Whip the cream with the water until it holds soft peaks, then whisk in the sweetened lemon juice. Turn the mixture into a shallow freezer tray, individual serving dishes or hollowed out lemons. Cover and still-freeze (page 4), without stirring, until firm.

RICH VANILLA ICE CREAM

Illustrated on pages 34/35

Condensed milk provides the sweetening in this very easily-made ice.

─────────── SERVES 6 ───────────

1¼ cups heavy cream, well chilled
¾ cup canned condensed milk, well chilled
real vanilla extract

───────────────────────────────

Put the cream and condensed milk into a bowl, add vanilla extract to taste, and whip until the mixture holds soft peaks. When adding the flavoring, remember that freezing will dull its intensity.

Turn the mixture into a shallow freezer tray, or into individual serving dishes. Cover and still-freeze (page 4), without stirring, until firm.

HONEY ICE CREAM WITH LAVENDER

Illustrated on pages 34/35

Lavender flowers are commonly used as a herb in the south of France, and pungent lavender-perfumed honey is sold from roadside stalls at the edges of purple cushioned fields.

─────────── SERVES 6 ───────────

½ cup lavender honey
1⅞ cups whipping cream
1 teaspoon fresh lavender flowers

───────────────────────────────

If the honey is thick, thin it down with a little of the cream. Whip the remaining cream until it holds soft peaks and fold in the honey and lavender flowers.

Turn the mixture into a shallow freezer tray or individual serving dishes. Cover and still-freeze (page 4) without stirring until firm.

BANANA ICE CREAM

Illustrated on page 39

A little of this rich banana ice cream goes a long way.

──────── SERVES 6 ────────

1 lb ripe bananas
1 cup confectioner's sugar
juice of 1 orange, or 3 tablespoons rum
1¼ cups heavy cream

Mash or process the peeled bananas with the icing sugar and orange juice or rum. Whip the cream until it holds soft peaks. Fold the banana purée into the cream.

Turn the mixture into a shallow freezer tray or individual serving dishes. Cover and still-freeze (page 4), without stirring, until firm.

RATAFIA ICE CREAM

Illustrated on page 39

Ratafia Biscuits are an excellent use for spare egg whites. They are easy to make (page 74) and excellent in ice cream as well as with it. This ice cream goes particularly well with a fruit sauce, such as raspberry or peach.

──────── SERVES 6 ────────

4 oz (¼ lb) Ratafia Biscuits (page 74)
1⅞ cups whipping cream
1 cup confectioner's sugar
almond or ratafia essence to taste

Crush the ratafias to coarse crumbs. Whip the cream with the icing sugar and a little almond or ratafia essence until it holds soft peaks. Fold in the crushed ratafias.

Turn the mixture into a shallow freezer tray or individual serving dishes. Cover and still-freeze (page 4), without stirring, until firm.

CHESTNUT ICE CREAM

A can of chestnut purée, sweetened and lightly flavored with vanilla, is a useful standby in any store-cupboard. As a variation on this easy ice cream recipe, stir a handful of broken meringue into the ice when it is partially frozen, then freeze until firm. It can be served sprinkled with flaked chocolate.

————— SERVES 6 —————

8 oz canned sweetened chestnut purée
2 tablespoons sweet sherry or milk
1¼ cups whipping cream
½ cup confectioner's sugar

Combine the chestnut purée with the sherry or milk, and mix to a smooth paste.

Whip the cream with the confectioner's sugar until it holds soft peaks, and fold it into the chestnut purée.

Turn the mixture into a shallow freezer tray or individual serving dishes. Cover and still-freeze (page 4), without stirring, until firm.

CHAZEL ICE CREAM

Chocolate and hazelnuts taste marvelous together — as confectioners have long appreciated — in this really speedy ice cream.

————— SERVES 6 —————

1⅞ cups whipping cream
4 oz chocolate and hazelnut spread
½ cup confectioner's sugar

Stir about 6 tablespoons of the cream into the chocolate and hazelnut spread. Whip the remaining cream with the icing sugar until it holds soft peaks. Fold the chocolate and hazelnut mixture into the cream.

Turn the mixture into a shallow freezer tray or individual serving dishes. Cover and still-freeze (page 4), without stirring, until firm.

Above: Chazel Ice Cream with Toar-drop Shortcake Thins (page 73).

Above: Ratafia Ice Cream (page 37) with Ratafia Biscuits (page 74).

Above: Banana Ice Cream (page 37).

Above: Chestnut Ice Cream.

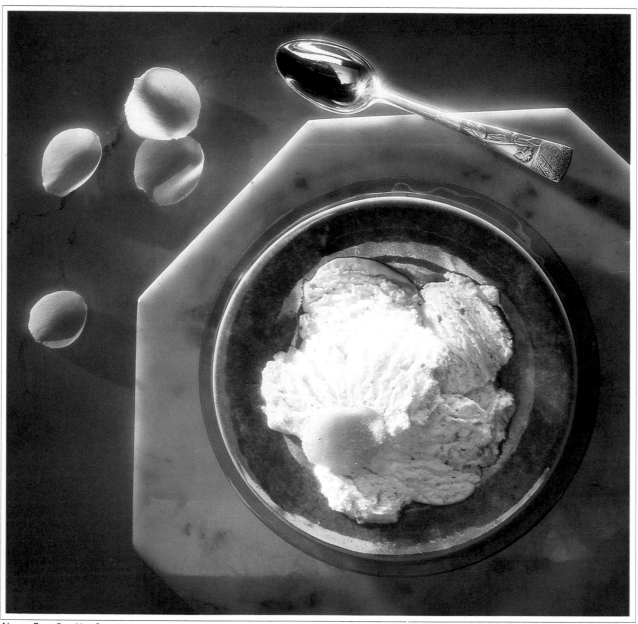

Above: Rose Petal Ice Cream.

ROSE PETAL ICE CREAM

Candied rose petals and rosewater perfume this romantic sounding ice. The strength of rosewater varies, so add a teaspoonful at a time and taste. It will look the part too if decorated with whole crystalized rose petals (page 78).

—————— SERVES 6 ——————

2 oz candied rose petals
1 cup confectioner's sugar
1⅞ cups heavy cream
rosewater to taste

Crush the candied rose petals almost to a powder. Combine the icing sugar with the cream and whisk until the mixture holds soft peaks. Fold in the candied rose petals and add rosewater a little at a time, bearing in mind that freezing will dull the flavoring.

Turn the mixture into a shallow freezer tray or individual serving dishes, and still-freeze (page 4), without stirring, until firm.

STRAWBERRY ICE CREAM

Illustration on page 43

Ripe fruit that is full of flavor is the essential ingredient of strawberry ice cream, and as long as damaged parts of the berries are discarded, there is no better use for less than perfect specimens. The orange and lemon juice helps to bring out the flavor of the strawberries. The same technique and recipe is also suitable for raspberries.

—————— SERVES 6 ——————

12 oz (¾ lb) ripe strawberries, hulled
juice of 1 orange
juice of 1 lemon
¾ cup sugar
1⅞ cups whipping cream

Rub the berries through a sieve, or process them briefly in a blender or food processor and strain the purée.

Combine the purée with the orange and lemon juice and sugar. Set the mixture aside for about 2 hours, stirring it from time to time until the sugar has dissolved completely. (This step intensifies the flavor of the fruit.)

Whip the cream until it holds soft peaks, combine it with the sweetened purée and whisk them lightly together.

Freeze in an ice cream machine following the manufacturer's instructions. Or still-freeze (page 4), vigorously whisking the partially frozen ice at least once during the freezing process.

DAMSON ICE CREAM

For flavor, damsons and greengages are the aristocrats of the plum family, and both make excellent ices. Damson ice cream is smooth, rich and assertively flavored.

--------- SERVES 6 ---------

1 lb damsons
½ cup packed brown sugar
1¼ cups water
4 egg yolks
1 cup confectioner's sugar
1¼ cups heavy cream
2 tablespoons iced water

Put the damsons into a saucepan with the brown sugar and 1¼ cups water and bring to a boil. Cover and simmer the fruit until it is tender, about 10 minutes depending on the ripeness of the damsons.

Press the stewed fruit through a sieve. Discard the stones and chill the purée in the refrigerator.

In a bowl set over a saucepan of simmering water, beat the egg yolks with the confectioner's sugar until the mixture is warm but not hot. Take the bowl off the heat and continue beating until the mixture has tripled its original volume, then chill it in the refrigerator.

Whisk the cream with the iced water until it holds soft peaks. Combine the damson purée, egg mixture and whipped cream and whisk them lightly together.

Freeze in an ice cream machine following the manufacturer's instructions. Or still-freeze (page 4), vigorously whisking the partially frozen ice at least once during the freezing process.

PRUNE ICE CREAM

Liberate the humble prune from its custard and sniggers schoolboy image by transforming it into this rich, grown-up ice. Prune ice cream is a worthy candidate for a slosh of optional alcohol. Almost any spirit, from gin to cognac, does the trick. Use Indian or China tea at normal strength for this recipe. You can use the same recipe to make a golden ice cream with dried apricots.

--------- SERVES 6 ---------

1 lb plump prunes
about 3¾ cups cold tea
rind of half an orange
½ cup packed brown sugar
1¼ cups whipping cream
2 tablespoons gin (optional)

Put the prunes into a bowl with the orange rind and add enough cold tea to cover them. Leave them to soak for several hours, preferably overnight, then add the sugar and simmer in a saucepan until tender. Set them aside until they are cool enough to handle.

Pit the prunes and discard the orange rind. Purée the fruit with its cooking syrup either by passing it through a sieve, or by processing it in a blender or food processor and then straining it. Stir in the gin, if used.

Whisk the cream until it holds soft peaks then combine it with the prune purée.

Freeze in an ice cream machine following the manufacturer's instructions. Or still-freeze (page 4), vigorously whisking the partially frozen ice at least once during the freezing process.

Top: Damson Ice Cream with langue du chat biscuits, center: Prune Ice Cream, below: Strawberry Ice Cream (page 41).

Above: Coconut Ice Cream

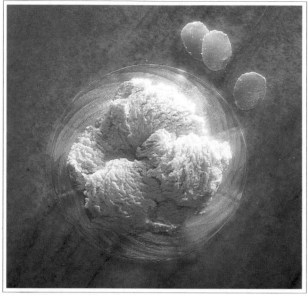

Above: Melon and Ginger Ice Cream.

Above: Mango Ice Cream.

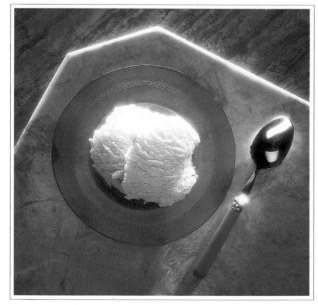

Above: Nectarine Ice Cream.

MELON AND GINGER ICE CREAM

A really ripe melon, one that is so heavily perfumed that its character is plain, will make a memorable ice cream.

―――― SERVES 6 ――――

1 ripe melon about 1 lb
juice of 1 lemon
¾ cup packed brown sugar
1¼ cups whipping cream
2 oz crystalized ginger, finely chopped

Halve the melon, discard the seeds and spoon out the flesh. Purée it by pressing it through a sieve, or by processing it in a blender or food processor and straining it. Add the lemon juice and sugar to the purée and leave the mixture to stand for about 2 hours, stirring it from time to time until the sugar has dissolved.

Whisk the cream until it holds soft peaks, then combine it with the melon purée and the ginger. Freeze in an ice cream machine following the manufacturer's instructions. Or still-freeze (page 4), vigorously whisking the partially frozen ice at least once during freezing.

MANGO ICE CREAM

Fully ripe mangoes are heavily perfumed, sumptuously flavored and quickly made into a rich ice cream. Perfectly ripe peaches and nectarines can also be used.

―――― SERVES 6 ――――

2 large ripe mangoes
juice of 1 lime or lemon
½ cup confectioner's sugar
1¼ cups whipping cream

Peel the mangoes and cut the flesh from the pits. Purée

the flesh with the lime or lemon juice either by processing it lightly in a blender or food processor, or by passing it through a sieve. Stir in the confectioner's sugar.

Whip the cream until it holds soft peaks. Whisk the purée lightly into the cream.

Freeze in an ice cream machine following the manufacturer's instructions. Or still-freeze (page 4), vigorously whisking the partially frozen ice at least once during the freezing process.

COCONUT ICE CREAM

Fresh coconut ices are made throughout the tropics. Dried coconut, too, gives excellent results.

―――― SERVES 6 ――――

3¾ cups milk
4 cups dried coconut
6 egg yolks
¾ cup sugar

Bring the milk to a boil in a saucepan and stir in the dried coconut. Set the mixture aside to infuse for at least 1 hour, then strain it through a fine sieve, pressing the coconut to extract most of the flavor.

Combine the egg yolks and sugar in a bowl. Whisk until the mixture is very pale and leaves a trail when the beaters are lifted. Gradually whisk in the coconut-flavored milk.

Return the mixture to the pan and cook it over a very low heat, or cook it in the top of a double boiler, stirring constantly until the custard is thick enough to coat the back of a wooden spoon.

Remove the custard from the heat to cool, stirring it from time to time to prevent a skin forming.

Freeze in an ice cream machine following the manufacturer's instructions. Or still-freeze (page 4), vigorously whisking the partially frozen ice at least once during the freezing process.

Top: Iced Caramel Mousse, below: Chocolate Marquise.

ICED CARAMEL MOUSSE

Use Ratafias (page 74) or amaretti biscuits for the crumb covering of this mousse.

―――――――― SERVES 6 ――――――――

1 cup sugar
juice of 1 lemon
1 tablespoon powdered gelatin
2 egg whites
a pinch of salt
1¼ cups heavy cream
1 cup graham cracker crumbs

Prepare a 2-lb loaf pan by lining it with baking parchment or foil.

Put the sugar and 6 tablespoons of water in a heavy saucepan and heat gently, stirring, until the sugar has dissolved completely. Wash down any crystals from the sides of the pan with a pastry brush dipped in cold water. Raise the heat and cook the sugar until it turns a rich golden brown. Watch it carefully because if it darkens too much the caramel will be bitter.

As soon as the caramel is sufficiently colored, take the pan off the heat and immediately dip its base in cold water to stop the temperature rising further. Stir in ⅔ cup water. The caramel will set hard on contact with the water, but will soon melt again with an occasional stir. Cool completely to a brown syrup.

Put the lemon juice into a small saucepan with 2 tablespoons of water and sprinkle the gelatin over it. Set it aside for a few minutes to let it swell and soften. Then heat very gently, without allowing it to boil, until the gelatin is completely melted. Stir the warm liquid gelatin into the caramel syrup and set it aside until it is cool and beginning to set.

Whisk the egg whites with a pinch of salt until they hold firm peaks. Whip the cream until it too holds firm peaks. Combine the caramel syrup with the whisked egg whites and cream and whisk them together lightly. Turn the mixture into the prepared loaf pan and freeze.

Remove the frozen mousse from the pan and strip off its lining papers. Allow the outside to soften a little, then press the graham cracker crumbs all over the surface. Return the dessert to the freezer until it is needed. If it is to be stored for more than an hour or two it should be covered to prevent ice crystals forming on it.

CHOCOLATE MARQUISE

Very rich and dark, a Chocolate Marquise is frozen in a brick-shaped loaf pan and sliced, straight from the freezer. Serve a slice on a plate which has been flooded with a layer of vanilla or coffee sauce – simply the custard bases of those ices, before freezing. Variations to a basic marquise can include broken meringue or rum-soaked raisins.

―――――――― SERVES 6 ――――――――

8 oz (½ lb) dark chocolate
½ cup (1 stick) unsalted butter, diced
2 large eggs, separated
a pinch of salt
¾ cup confectioner's sugar
for the decoration
dark-roast coffee beans

Grate or break the chocolate into a bowl and add the butter. Heat gently over a pan of simmering water, stirring until the mixture is smooth.

In a second bowl whisk the egg whites with the salt until they hold stiff peaks. In a third bowl beat the egg yolks with the sugar until the mix is pale and fluffy.

Mix the melted chocolate lightly into the yolk mixture, then fold in the whisked whites. Spoon the mixture into a non-stick 2-lb loaf pan, cover the top with foil and freeze until firm.

To serve, turn the marquise onto a chilled serving plate. Decorate the top with a few glossy coffee beans.

Left: Passion Fruit Parfait, right: Liqueur Parfaits.

LIQUEUR PARFAITS

Parfaits are rich, smooth ices. They are often flavored with liqueurs and frozen in individual serving dishes. Stemmed colored glasses also make pretty containers. Or the rims of plain glasses can be frosted with plain or colored sugar. For orange sugar frosting to go with a Cointreau or Grand Marnier parfait, dip the rims of the glasses first in undiluted frozen orange juice then immediately into granulated sugar. Chill them until needed. If you are using tall glasses, check that they have room to stand in the freezer.

—————— SERVES 6 ——————

1 cup sugar
6 tablespoons water
4 egg yolks
4 tablespoons liqueur
2 egg whites
1 cup whipping cream

Put the sugar into a small, heavy saucepan with the water and heat gently, stirring, until the sugar has dissolved completely. Wash down any sugar crystals from the sides of the pan with a pastry brush dipped in cold water, then raise the heat and boil the syrup until it is just beginning to color (about 310°F on a candy thermometer).

Take the pan off the heat and set it aside to cool for 1 minute. In the meantime, put the egg yolks into a large bowl and whisk them to a froth. Gradually whisk in the hot syrup, and when it has been added, continue whisking until the mixture is cool and has tripled its original volume. Whisk in the liqueur, then chill the mixture in the refrigerator.

Whisk the egg whites until they hold stiff peaks. Whip the cream until it holds soft peaks. Combine the yolk mixture with the whisked egg whites and cream and whisk them together lightly. Turn the parfait into individual dishes and freeze until firm.

PASSION FRUIT PARFAIT

Passion fruit has a strong flavor and perfume which can stand dilution with eggs and cream. The ripe fruit look most unpromising, but until the skins are withered their perfume will be less than its best. To extract the flesh, open passion fruit like soft boiled eggs and spoon out the seedy interiors. Freeze the parfait in individual glasses, or in a decorative ice cream mold.

—————— SERVES 6 ——————

4 ripe passion fruit
1 cup granulated sugar
6 tablespoons water
4 egg yolks
2 egg whites
1 cup whipping cream

Sieve the passion fruit pulp to extract the seeds. The amount of juice left to flavor the parfait will be small, but powerful.

Put the sugar and water into a small, heavy saucepan and heat gently, stirring, until the sugar has dissolved completely. Wash down any crystals from the sides of the pan with a pastry brush dipped in cold water. Raise the heat and boil the syrup until it is just beginning to colour (about 310°F on a candy thermometer).

Take the pan off the heat and set it aside to cool for 1 minute. While it is cooling, put the egg yolks into a large bowl and whisk them to a froth. Gradually whisk in the hot syrup, and when it has all been added, continue whisking until the mixture is cool and has tripled its original volume. Whisk in the strained passion fruit juice, then chill the mixture in the refrigerator.

Whisk the egg whites until they hold stiff peaks. Whip the cream until it holds soft peaks. Then combine the yolk mixture with the whisked egg whites and cream and whisk them together lightly.

Turn the parfait into individual dishes or into a mold and freeze until firm. Serve on its own or with a fresh Fruit Coulis (page 77), such as a mango purée.

ICED RASPBERRY SOUFFLE

Iced soufflés are every bit as dramatic as the hot kind and involve no strain on the cook's nervous system. An iced soufflé cannot flop. Raspberries are ideal for this type of soufflé because their flavor survives dispersal through a cloud of whipped cream and meringue.

———————————— SERVES 6 ————————————

12 oz (¾ lb) ripe raspberries, fresh or frozen and thawed
½ cup sugar
2 tablespoons orange liqueur, or fresh orange juice
2 egg whites
½ cup confectioner's sugar
1⅞ cups whipping cream

Wrap a strip of double thickness baking parchment or oiled greaseproof paper around the outside of a straight-sided 1 quart soufflé dish, or around 6 individual ramekins. The paper should come 2 in above the rim of the dish, or dishes, to make a collar. Secure the join with a pin, and chill the dish, or dishes.

Set aside a dozen perfect raspberries to decorate the finished soufflé. Purée the remaining raspberries either by pressing the fruit through a fine sieve to remove the seeds, or by processing them briefly in a blender or food processor and straining the pulp. Stir in the sugar and orange liqueur (or juice). Set aside for at least 1 hour to allow the flavor to develop, stirring from time to time until the sugar has dissolved.

Whisk the egg whites until they hold soft peaks then add the sugar and whisk until the mixture holds firm peaks. Whip the cream until it holds soft peaks.

Whisk the purée, whisked egg whites and cream together lightly and immediately turn the mixture into the prepared dish or dishes. Smooth the top and cover with foil – keeping it away from the top of the soufflé – and freeze until firm.

Remove the foil and the paper collar before ripening the soufflé to serve it. Decorate the top with the reserved raspberries.

ICED PEAR SOUFFLE

Illustrated on page 52

Poire William eau-de-vie underlines the pear flavor in this lovely, light, iced soufflé. Use the same recipe to make other flavors with fresh fruits and their own fruit-flavored liqueurs. Or use a little kirsch instead.

———————————— SERVES 6 ————————————

1 lb dessert or cooking pears, peeled and cored
juice of 1 lemon
1¼ cup heavy cream
4 tablespoons Poire William eau-de-vie or kirsch
1 cooked Meringue (page 76)

Wrap a strip of double thickness baking parchment or oiled greaseproof paper around the outside of a straight-sided 1 quart soufflé dish, or around 6 individual ramekins. The paper should come 2 in above the rim of the dish, or dishes, to make a collar. Secure the join with a pin, and chill the dish, or dishes, until they are needed.

Chop the pears roughly and turn the pieces in the lemon juice to prevent them from discoloring. Cook them until tender in a stainless steel or enamelled saucepan with a little water, if needed. Or bake the pears, covered, in a moderate oven (350°F). Timing will depend on the ripeness of the pears.

Cool the cooked pears and purée them either by passing them through a sieve, or by processing them in a blender or food processor. Set the purée aside to cool.

Whip the cream with the eau-de-vie (or kirsch) until it holds soft peaks. Combine the pear purée with the meringue and whipped cream and whisk them together lightly. Turn the mixture into the prepared dish, or dishes and cover with foil. Freeze until firm.

Remove the foil lid and the paper collar before ripening the soufflé to serve it. Spoonfuls of the soufflé may also be served in Tuile or Brandy Snap Baskets (page 72/73).

Above: Iced Raspberry Soufflé.

Top: Zabaglione Semi Freddo, center: Iced Pear Soufflé (page 50), below: Iced Maple Pecan Soufflé in Tuile Basket (page 72).

ZABAGLIONE SEMI FREDDO

Zabaglione is the simplest of spectacular desserts – just egg yolks, sugar and marsala, for which a medium or sweet sherry may be substituted at a pinch. In its warm form, zabaglione has to be made just before it is served. But this iced version is a more practical proposition for entertaining.

––––––––––– SERVES 6 –––––––––––

4 egg yolks
½ cup sugar
⅔ cup dry marsala
⅔ cup whipping cream

Put the egg yolks into a fairly large bowl (ideally made of copper) which will fit over a pan. Add the sugar and whisk until the mixture is very pale and falls back leaving a trail when the beaters are lifted.

Whisk in the marsala, then set the bowl over a pan of simmering water and continue whisking until the mixture has at least doubled its volume. Take off the heat and set the bowl in cold water, or over ice, and whisk until the mixture is cool.

Whip the cream until it holds soft peaks. Combine it with the cold zabaglione and whisk them together lightly.

Turn the mixture into small stemmed glasses or individual dishes and freeze until firm. Serve with crisp, buttery Classic Tuiles (page 72).

ICED MAPLE PECAN SOUFFLE

Real maple syrup tastes so much better than the cheaper synthetic kind that it is worth searching out. It keeps almost indefinitely which is more than can be said of pecans or any other nuts for that matter. The oil in old or badly stored nuts gradually turns rancid, so it is a good idea to taste shelled nuts before using them in a recipe.

––––––––––– SERVES 6 –––––––––––

1 tablespoon powdered gelatin
4 tablespoons water
½ cup maple syrup
3 eggs, separated
a pinch of salt
½ cup confectioner's sugar
1⅞ cups heavy cream
½ cup shelled pecans, chopped
for the decoration
pecan halves

Wrap a strip of double thickness baking parchment or oiled greaseproof paper around the outside of a straight-sided 1 quart soufflé dish, or around 6 individual ramekins. The paper should come 2 in above the rim of the dish, or dishes, to make a collar. Secure the join with a pin, and chill the dish, or dishes.

Sprinkle the gelatin over the water in a small pan and set it aside for a few minutes until the gelatin has softened and swollen. Heat very gently, stirring, without allowing it to boil, until the gelatin has melted completely. Set aside.

Put the maple syrup and egg yolks into a bowl over a pan of simmering water and whisk until the mixture is lukewarm. Take the bowl off the heat and continue whisking until the mixture is cool and has tripled its original volume.

In a second bowl whisk the egg whites with a pinch of salt, until they are foamy, then add the confectioner's sugar and whisk until the mixture holds stiff peaks. >

< In a third bowl whip the cream until it holds soft peaks.

Combine the gelatin with the yolk mixture, whisked egg whites and whipped cream and whisk them together lightly. Fold in the chopped pecans and turn the mixture into the prepared dish or dishes. Cover with a lid of foil – keeping it away from the top of the soufflé – and freeze until firm.

Remove the foil and the paper collar before ripening the soufflé to serve it. Top with the pecan halves.

If there is time for last-minute messing around, dip the decorative nuts in liquid caramel (½ cup sugar cooked with 4 tablespoons water until golden brown) and set them on a greased surface to cool and harden.

KNICKERBOCKER GLORY

King of sundaes is the one and only Knickerbocker Glory. It has an extravagance that appeals to the child in the staidest adult and one of the few places still serving the genuine article is the Soda Fountain at Fortnum and Mason in London's Piccadilly.
The glass for a Knickerbocker Glory should be tall and fluted like a giant ice cream cone. It is then filled to brimming with ices, fruit and cream.

--- FOR 1 SERVING ---

sugared raspberries
crushed pineapple
1 scoop Vanilla Ice Cream (page 24)
1 scoop Strawberry Ice Cream (page 41)
1 tablespoon whipped cream, or to taste
a maraschino or glacé cherry

Put a little of the fruit in the bottom of the glass and top with the ices and remaining fruit in any order. Pipe a generous dollop of whipped cream on top and crown with the cherry.

Left: Knickerbocker Glory, center: Nutcase (page 56), right: Big
Business (page 56), with a florentine wafer and pompadour fan wafers.

SUNDAES – SIX OF THE BEST

Sundaes do not have to be fancy or festooned with cream to succeed. One of the best is the simplest I know. In France the classic combination of lemon sorbet and iced vodka is called 'le colonel' and it is as subtle and sophisticated an ice as you will meet.

Coupe Cassis: another perennially popular combination of ices and fruit, in this case black currants. In a glass or dish combine a scoop of Vanilla Ice Cream (page 24) with a scoop of Black Currant Sorbet (page 16) and fresh or lightly stewed black currants. Add a tablespoon of black currant alcohol (crème de cassis) or syrup, and top with Chantilly Cream (page 76).

Big Business: a scoop of Chocolate Ice Cream (page 31), another of Chocolate Chip Ice Cream (page 24) and a spoonful each of Hot Chocolate Sauce and Chocolate Fudge Sauce (page 77).

English Garden: a scoop of Apple and Honey Sorbet (page 6), another of Apple and Calvados Sorbet (page 20) served with Raspberry Coulis (page 77) and topped with red berries, whichever are in season.

Tippler: Rum and Raisin Ice Cream (page 24) with broken Ratafia Biscuits (page 74), Raspberry Coulis (page 77), Jaeger Tea Sorbet (page 23) and a Chantilly Cream topping (page 76).

Nutcase: scoops of Praline (page 27), Chocolate and Burnt Almond (page 31) and Ratafia (page 37) Ice Creams with fresh Mango Coulis (page 77), Chantilly Cream (page 76) and a dusting of Powdered Praline (page 27).

Left: Fatless Tuiles (page 72), center: English Garden
with Red Currant Fruit Coulis (page 77), right: Coupe Cassis with
Black Currant Fruit Coulis (page 77).

ICE CREAM BOMBES

Fancy ices were the height of fashion at the turn of the century. In The Complete Guide to the Art of Modern Cookery, first published in 1902, the great chef Auguste Escoffier offers 77 recipes for ice cream bombes in a list that marches the length of the alphabet from Bombe Aboukir to Bombe Zamora by way of Bombes Frou-Frou, Hilda, Mathilde, Odette, Rosette and Tosca.
A point to remember when constructing a bombe — usually in a tall metal dome, but a pudding bowl will do — is to put the softest ice in the center. This avoids a melting exterior with a rock hard core.
Parfaits (page 49) and many of the quick, still-frozen ices (pages 35-41) are suitable for bombe centers. Or there is the following classic Basic Bombe Mousse which can be flavored in numerous ways.

BASIC BOMBE MOUSSE

—— SERVES 6 ——

½ cup sugar
½ cup water
4 egg yolks
flavoring essence to taste

Put the sugar and water into a saucepan and heat gently until the sugar has dissolved completely. Wash down any sugar crystals from the sides of the pan with a pastry brush dipped in cold water. Raise the heat and boil the syrup, not too briskly, for about five minutes.

Put the egg yolks into a fairly large bowl and, whisking steadily, gradually add the syrup. Continue whisking until the mixture is thick and pale and about three times its original volume.

Set the bowl in cold water, or over ice, and whisk until the mousse is cold. Whisk in the flavoring. Cover and chill until needed. Keeps up to a week.

BOMBE ABOUKIR

This is the first of Escoffier's named bombes, a classic combination of pistachio ice cream and praline flavored bombe mousse. Adjust the quantities of ice cream and bombe mousse to fit the mold, allowing a total of approximately 1 quart ⅜ cups for 6 ample servings.

—— SERVES 6 ——

2½ cups Cardamom and Pistachio Ice Cream (page 28)
¼ cup blanched almonds
⅛ cup sugar
½ cup heavy cream
1¼ cups Basic Bombe Mousse (left)

Chill the bombe mold well in the freezer. Ripen the pistachio ice cream in the refrigerator (page 5) until it is soft enough to be spooned. Line the mold with a layer of the pistachio ice cream, shaping it in an even layer right up to the rim. Cover the mold and freeze until the ice cream is firm again.

Use the almonds and sugar to make a praline as described on page 27, and grind the praline finely. Whip the cream until it holds soft peaks, then combine the bombe mousse, cream and powdered praline.

Spoon this mixture into the lined bombe mold, filling it completely. Cover and freeze until firm.

To serve the bombe, remove the lid and invert the mold on to a plate while it is still frozen hard. Wring out a cloth in hot water and use it to wrap the mold. Then holding the plate and mold together firmly, shake the bombe out of its container. Return the bombe to the freezer if not required immediately, or refrigerate it to ripen (page 5), as required, after smoothing over the surface if necessary and mopping up any drips.

Above: Bombe Aboukir.

ASSORTED BOMBES

The first bombes were frozen in spherical molds and the name has stuck despite the move to dome-shaped ices and other variations.

Obviously there is no limit, except that of space, to the number of layers or flavors a bombe may have — which makes them a useful way to present ice cream leftovers elegantly.

Every cook will quickly find favorite combinations of flavors. But for any one in need of further inspiration, here is a description of the ices Escoffier named after all those girls.

Bombe Frou-Frou: Vanilla Ice Cream (page 24) filled with rum-flavored Bombe Mousse (page 58) dotted with crystalized fruits.

Bombe Hilda: Hazelnut Ice Cream (page 27) filled with chartreuse-flavored Bombe Mousse (page 58) containing Hazelnut Praline (page 27).

Bombe Mathilde: Kirsch-flavored ice cream (Vanilla Ice Cream base, page 24, flavored with 3 tablespoons kirsch) filled with apricot-flavored Bombe Mousse (page 58). Use a strongly flavored purée of dried apricots in place of half the usual quantity of cream.

Bombe Odette: Vanilla Ice Cream (page 24) filled with praline-flavored Bombe Mousse (page 58).

Bombe Rosette: Vanilla Ice Cream (page 24) filled with Chantilly Cream (page 76) containing fresh red currants.

Bombe Tosca: Apricot Ice Cream (see the variation on Prune Ice Cream, page 42) filled with maraschino-flavored Bombe Mousse (page 58) containing diced fruit.

Left: Bombe Rosette, right: Bombe Tosca

BOMBE ZAMORA

The final bombe in Escoffier's ice cream alphabet is lined with coffee ice cream and filled with orange curaçao-flavored mousse. Alternative orange flavored liqueurs include Grand Marnier and Cointreau.

—————— SERVES 6 ——————

2½ cups Coffee Ice Cream (page 31)
½ cup heavy cream
3 tablespoons orange curaçao
1¼ cups Basic Bombe Mousse (page 58)

Chill the bombe mold well in the freezer. Ripen the coffee ice cream (page 5) until it is soft enough to be spooned. Line the mold with a layer of coffee ice cream keeping the thickness as even as possible right up to the rim. Cover and freeze until the ice cream is firm, again.

Whip the cream with the curaçao until it holds soft peaks then whisk it lightly into the bombe mousse. Spoon this mixture into the lined bombe mold, filling it completely. Cover and freeze it until firm.

To serve the bombe, remove the lid and invert the mold on to a plate while it is still frozen hard. Wring out a cloth in hot water and use it to wrap the mold. Then holding the plate and mold together firmly, shake the bombe out of its container. Return the bombe to the freezer if not required immediately, or refrigerate it to ripen (page 5), after smoothing over the surface if necessary and mopping up any drips.

BAKED ALASKA

Illustrated on page 67

Baked Alaska is one of the minor wonders of the world — ice cream straight from the oven in a coat of warm meringue appears to defy common sense. The trick, for so it appears, is that the thousands of tiny air bubbles in the meringue effectively insulate the ice cream for the short time it is in the oven.
Whatever flavor of ice cream you choose, freeze it in a brick-shaped mould. A plastic freezer box is ideal because it allows the ice cream to be unmolded without dipping the container in hot water. Never ripen (page 5) ice cream when making Baked Alaska.
The cake base should be about ½ in thick, the same shape as the ice cream brick and about ½ in wider all round. Use the Chocolate Cake recipe on page 65, baking it on a jelly roll tray and cutting it to fit. Alternatively, use any other plain sponge cake. The meringue may be the cooked Meringue Layer described on page 76, or the easy recipe below.

—————— SERVES 6 ——————

1 brick Cassata Ice Cream (page 24)
1 cake base (follow recipe given for Chocolate Ice Cream Cake, page 65)
3 egg whites
¼ cup sugar

Heat the oven to 450°F.

Place the cake base on a baking sheet and position the ice cream on top of it. Put them in the freezer while making the meringue.

Whisk the egg whites until they hold soft peaks, then whisk in the sugar, a little at a time, until the meringue is thick and glossy and holds firm peaks.

Spoon or pipe the meringue in an even layer over the top and sides of the ice cream and cover the sides of the cake as well.

Bake in the oven for about 5 minutes, to just brown the meringue lightly. Serve at once.

Above: Bombe Zamora.

Above: Chocolate Ice Cream Cake.

CHOCOLATE ICE CREAM CAKE

Mostly ice cream and not too much cake is the right formula for ice cream cakes of any flavor. Rich ices that neither freeze too hard nor melt as soon as you look at them are the ones to choose for cake making.

―――――――――― SERVES 20 ――――――――――

for the cake
4 eggs
½ cup sugar
½ cup flour
¼ cup cocoa
1 teaspoon baking powder
1 × 12-in Meringue layer (page 76)
for the filling
3¼ cups Chocolate Ice Cream (page 31)
3¼ cups Chazel Ice Cream (page 38)
3¼ cups Chocolate Marquise (see page 47)
for the decoration
⅔ cup sweetened condensed milk
4 oz (¼ lb) dark chocolate, broken up
1¼ cups whipping cream

Heat the oven to 400°F.

To make the cake, beat the eggs with the sugar until the mixture is pale and thick, and falls back leaving a trail when the beaters are lifted.

Sift together the flour, cocoa and baking powder and fold them into the egg mixture. Turn the mixture into a 12-in round spring form cake pan lined with baking parchment and bake it for about 15 minutes or until a skewer inserted into the center comes out clean.

Leave the cake to cool in its pan for 10 minutes before turning it onto a wire rack and stripping off the lining paper. When it is quite cold split it into 3 layers.

To assemble the cake, put the first cake layer on a flat serving plate or base, checking first that the freezer door will shut behind it. Spread the cake with the chazel ice cream which has been partially frozen, or if made earlier, ripened to a spreadable consistency (page 5).

Top with the meringue and freeze until firm.

Spread a layer of partially frozen or softened chocolate marquise over the meringue and top with the second cake layer. Freeze until firm.

Spread a layer of partially frozen or ripened chocolate ice cream over the cake and top with the last cake layer. Freeze until firm.

To make the frosting, heat the condensed milk and chocolate in a saucepan, stirring, until the chocolate has melted. Allow to cool, then chill in the refrigerator.

Whisk the chilled chocolate mixture vigorously to lighten it. Whip the cream until it holds soft peaks, then combine it with the chocolate mixture, whisking them together lightly.

Spread the top and sides of the cake with the chocolate cream. This can be finished in one of two ways: either pull it into frosted peaks using the tip of a rounded knife; or smooth it completely and comb it with wavy lines, using a clean coarse-toothed comb.

Freeze the cake just long enough to firm the icing, then cover it and freeze until firm.

65

STRAWBERRY ICE CREAM CAKE

*Layers of meringue sandwiched with fresh Strawberry
and Lemon Ice Creams make an ice cream cake that
can be decorated at the last minute with fresh fruit.*

SERVES 12

4×9-in Meringue layers (page 76)
1 recipe Strawberry Ice Cream (page 41)
1 recipe Lemon Ice Cream (page 35)
for the decoration
fresh strawberries

Place a meringue layer on a flat plate on which the cake
can be frozen and later served. Spread it with half the
partially frozen or ripened (page 5) strawberry ice cream
and top with another meringue layer. Freeze until firm.

Spread with approximately one-third of the partially
frozen or ripened lemon ice cream and top with another
meringue layer. Freeze until firm.

To complete the assembly, spread the remaining
strawberry ice cream over the meringue and top with
the last meringue layer. Freeze until firm.

Finally ice the cake with the remaining lemon ice
cream, giving it a smooth or peaked finish. A smoothly
iced cake can be combed (see previous recipe) or decorated like a conventionally iced cake with slightly
sweetened whipped cream. Allow ¼ cup confectioner's sugar to every ⅔ cup heavy cream. Because cream
holds its shape less well than most icings, elaborate
decorations are not advisable. Freeze the cake until firm
before covering it for freezer storage. Decorate with
strawberries.

Left: Baked Alaska (page 62),
right: Strawberry Ice Cream Cake.

Left: Carob Ice Cream, right: Honey Yogurt Ice with delice biscuits.

HONEY YOGURT ICE

Plain yogurt sweetened with honey makes the simplest of ices. The richer the yogurt and the sweeter the ice, the easier it is to achieve a smooth texture. So if using low-fat yogurt and little honey 2 or 3 beatings may be required during freezing.

— SERVES 6 —

3¼ cups plain yogurt
6 tablespoons strongly perfumed honey

Stir the honey into the yogurt, adding more honey if the mixture is not sweet enough.

Freeze in an ice cream machine following the manufacturer's instructions. Or still-freeze (page 4), vigorously whisking the partially frozen ice several times during the freezing process.

CAROB ICE CREAM

Carob powder is a useful substitute for cocoa in recipes where the taste of chocolate is wanted without the side effects experienced by some migraine sufferers and others sensitive to substances in cocoa. Carob powder is widely available in health food shops.

— SERVES 6 —

6 egg yolks
1 cup packed brown sugar
4 tablespoons carob powder
3¼ cups milk
vanilla extract to taste

Whisk the egg yolks with the sugar until pale and fluffy, then whisk in the carob powder. Gradually whisk in the milk.

Cook the custard, heating it gently in a heavy sauce pan over a very low heat, or cook it in the top of a double boiler, stirring constantly until the custard is thick enough to coat the back of a wooden spoon.

Remove the custard from the heat and set it aside to cool, stirring it from time to time to prevent a skin forming. Then add vanilla extract to taste, remembering that the flavor will fade with freezing.

Freeze in an ice cream machine following the manufacturer's instructions. Or still-freeze (page 4), vigorously whisking the partially frozen ice at least once during the freezing process.

STRAWBERRY SORBET

Ripe fruit has its own sugars which make it unnecessary, for taste reasons, to add more. Using an ice cream machine which freezes and churns simultaneously, puréed soft fruits or freshly squeezed orange juice need only to be frozen to make acceptable sorbets.
Without the help of sugar or an ice cream machine to inhibit the formation of ice crystals, the addition of a little gelatin helps to smooth ices made by hand.

—————————— SERVES 6 ——————————

1 lb ripe strawberries, hulled
1¼ cups fresh orange juice
1 tablespoon powdered gelatin
3 tablespoons water

Purée the strawberries by pressing them through a sieve, or by processing them lightly in a blender or food processor and straining the purée. Stir in the orange juice and set the mixture aside for about 2 hours to allow the flavor to develop.

Sprinkle the gelatin over the water in a small saucepan. Set it aside for a few minutes to swell and soften, then heat it gently, without allowing it to boil, stirring until the gelatin has dissolved completely. Allow it to cool a little, then stir the liquid gelatin into the fruit purée.

Freeze in an ice cream machine following the manufacturer's instructions. Or still-freeze (page 4), vigorously whisking the partially frozen ice at least once during the freezing process.

VANILLA ICE

Low-fat, low-sugar ices need special care in the making if the result is to be pleasing. It is with these mixtures that a machine which whisks and freezes simultaneously is such a boon. Frequent whisking to break down the size of the ice crystals is the answer when making this kind of ice by hand.

—————————— SERVES 6 ——————————

3¼ cups skimmed milk
1 vanilla pod, split lengthways
2 tablespoons cornstarch
½ cup packed brown sugar
1 tablespoon powdered gelatin
3 tablespoons water

Put the milk and vanilla pod into a saucepan and bring to a boil. Immediately take off the heat, and set aside to cool. When it is quite cold, remove the vanilla pod which can be washed and dried and used again.

Mix the cornstarch with the sugar and stir in a little of the milk to make a smooth paste. Reheat the remaining milk to boiling point and gradually stir it into the cornstarch and sugar mixture. Return the custard to the pan and cook, stirring, until it has thickened. Simmer for 5 minutes, then take off the heat and leave to cool.

In the meantime, sprinkle the gelatin over the water in a small saucepan. Set it aside for a few minutes to swell and soften, then heat very gently without allowing it to boil, stirring until the gelatin has dissolved completely. Stir the liquid gelatin into the cool custard.

Freeze in an ice cream machine following the manufacturer's instructions. Or still-freeze (page 4), vigorously whisking the partially frozen ice two or three times during the freezing process.

Top: Strawberry Sorbet, below: Vanilla Ice with Tuiles (page 72).

FATLESS TUILES
Illustrated on pages 74/75

Fragile biscuit baskets are attractive containers for ices. This fatless version of the classic recipe was evolved by Anton Mosimann for the style of cooking he has called cuisine naturelle. The same mixture can be rolled, while it is still warm and pliable, round the handle of a wooden spoon to make cigarette biscuits. Smaller tuiles can be molded in a gentle curve over a rolling pin or shaped into cornets around cream horn molds.

—————— MAKES ABOUT 8 BASKETS ——————

1 cup confectioner's sugar, sifted
1½ cups flour
6 large egg whites
a pinch of salt
finely grated rind of 3 oranges
½ cup flaked almonds

Mix together the confectioner's sugar, flour, egg whites and salt to make a thick, smooth batter. Strain the batter if necessary, to remove any lumps.

Add the orange rind and almonds and set the mixture aside for 2 hours.

Heat the oven to 350°F.

Using your fingers, spread half the mixture into 4 rough 7-in circles on non-stick baking sheets. Bake for about 8 minutes, until golden.

Lift the biscuits from the trays one at a time and immediately drape each circle over a well-oiled inverted cup or small tumbler. The warm biscuits will droop into a rough basket shape. As the tuiles cool, they become firm and crisp. If any harden before they have been molded, they can be softened again in the oven.

Bake and mold the remaining mixture in the same way.

Tuiles quickly become soggy when exposed to damp air, so as soon as they are quite cold, store them in an airtight container.

CLASSIC TUILES
Illustrated on pages 74/75

This conventional recipe for tuiles contains butter. The newly baked biscuits can be molded in the same ways as described in the previous recipe.

—————— MAKES ABOUT 50 ——————

½ cup (1 stick) butter, softened
½ cup sugar
5 large egg whites
vanilla extract
¾ cup plain flour

Heat the oven to 400°F.

Cream the butter in a mixing bowl, add the sugar and beat until the mixture is pale and fluffy. Beat in the egg whites, a little at a time, and a few drops of vanilla extract, then fold in the flour.

Pipe or spoon small mounds of the mixture onto well-greased baking sheets, spacing them well apart so that they have room to spread. Bake for about 10 minutes, or until they are pale gold in the center and darker at the edges.

Cool the tuiles on a wire rack and as soon as they are quite cold, store them in an airtight container.

BRANDY SNAP BASKETS

Illustrated on pages 74/75

Brandy snaps can be molded into baskets, making crisp containers for creamy ices. Bake the snaps a few at a time and mold them while they are still hot from the oven over inverted cups or tumblers which have been well oiled or buttered.

―――――――― MAKES ABOUT 6 ――――――――

¼ cup (½ stick) butter
¼ cup sugar
2 tablespoons molasses
6 tablespoons flour
a pinch of salt
½ teaspoon ground ginger
1 teaspoon lemon juice
1 teaspoon brandy

Heat the oven to 325°F and line a baking sheet with baking parchment or buttered greaseproof paper.

Heat the butter, sugar and molasses in a small saucepan until the mixture is warm and melted but not hot. Sift together the flour, salt and ginger and stir them into the liquid butter mixture. Stir in the brandy and lemon juice.

Drop 2-tablespoonful blobs of batter, 4 at a time, onto the prepared baking sheet, spacing them well apart. Bake for 8-10 minutes, or until they are brown and bubbling.

Remove from the oven and allow the brandy snaps to cool on the tray for about 1 minute before lifting them, one at a time, and draping them over well-oiled inverted cups or tumblers. As the biscuits dry they become brittle and firm.

Bake and mold the remaining mixture in the same way.

SHORTCAKE THINS

Illustrated on pages 74/75

Melting shortcake cookies eat well with any ice.

―――――――― MAKES ABOUT 50 ――――――――

6 tablespoons (¾ stick) butter, softened
¾ cup sugar
1 egg yolk
finely grated rind of 1 lemon (optional)
1¼ cups flour

Heat the oven to 350°F.

Cream the butter in a mixing bowl, add the sugar and beat until the mixture is pale and fluffy. Beat in the egg yolk and lemon rind if used, then work in the flour and salt to make a stiff dough. Chill the dough in the refrigerator for about 30 minutes.

Roll out the dough to a thickness of about 3/16 in and use plain or fancy cutters to stamp out the biscuits. Arrange them on greased and floured baking sheets and bake for about 10 minutes, or until pale gold.

Cool the cookies on a wire rack and as soon as they are quite cold, store them in an airtight container.

RATAFIAS

Ratafias, like tuiles, are a useful recipe for using up spare egg whites after making custard based ices. These old fashioned almond cookies can be served with ices, or crushed and incorporated into them.

MAKES ABOUT 100

5 large egg whites
2¼ cups ground almonds
3 cups confectioner's sugar
almond or ratafia essence

Heat the oven to 300°F.

Whisk the egg whites until they hold stiff peaks, then fold in the ground almonds, sugar and essence to taste. Mix well to make a soft, sticky dough.

Pipe the mixture in small mounds (a teaspoonful or less) onto baking sheets lined with edible rice paper or non-stick baking parchment. Space the ratafias to allow a little spreading.

Bake for about 45 minutes, or until they are a pale, pinkish brown.

Leave the ratafias on the papers to cool on a wire rack. When they are quite cold, peel off the baking parchment, or trim the rice paper neatly round each ratafia.

Ratafias keep well for several weeks if stored in an airtight tin.

Clockwise, from top left: Meringue Basket (page 76), Fatless and Classic Tuiles (page 72), Brandy Snap Basket (page 73), Crystalized Flowers (page 78), Ice Cream with Mango Fruit Coulis (page 77), Shortcake Thins (page 73) and Ratafias.

MERINGUE

Illustrated on pages 74/75

For meringue nests, and for layers that can be built into all manner of iced desserts, meringue made with hot sugar syrup gives better results than egg whites whisked with loose sugar. All types of meringue keep well once baked, but this one is quite stable before it is dried. It can be stored for several days in the refrigerator, and a spoonful or two used when needed to lighten a sorbet or whipped cream.
Copper bowls really do produce more and stronger meringue from fewer egg whites. The reason is a reaction between the metal and a component of egg. To maximize this effect always use a balloon whisk with a copper bowl. When using an electric whisk, use a narrow, straight-sided bowl, and in either case, make sure that the utensils are clean and dry, and that the egg whites are at room temperature.

———— **MAKES 6 NESTS OR 2 9-in LAYERS** ————

1 cup sugar
⅔ cup water
4 egg whites

Put the sugar and water into a small saucepan and heat until the sugar has dissolved completely. Raise the heat and boil the syrup to the hard ball stage (about 250°F, on a candy thermometer). To test without a thermometer, drop a little of the syrup into iced water then roll into a ball with your fingers. When the cold plunge firms the syrup sufficiently to roll it into a tough lump, it has reached the hard ball stage.

While the syrup is boiling, whisk the egg whites until they hold stiff peaks. Whisking continuously, gradually add the hot sugar syrup. Continue whisking until the meringue is cold.

To make meringue nests, line one or more baking sheets with baking parchment and mark on them 6 circles about 3½ in in diameter.

Heat the oven to 225°F.

Spoon large mounds of meringue on to the sheets, and use the back of the spoon to spread it into circles. Make a shallow depression on top of each mound.

Alternatively, fit a large piping bag with a plain nozzle at least ½-in in diameter. Fill the bag with meringue and pipe circular bases, filling in the outlines from the center outwards. Then pipe two neat circles, one on top of the other, around the edge of the bases.

Bake the meringues in the oven for about 3 hours. Check from time to time, and if the meringues begin to color, reduce the heat still further.

To make meringue layers, mark prepared baking sheets with 2 large circles about 9 in in diameter. Pipe a single layer of meringue, filling each circle from the center outwards. Alternatively, divide the meringue between the two outlines and spread it out evenly, using a spatula, to fill the circles.

Bake the layers at the same temperature as nests.

CHANTILLY CREAM

Lighter and sweeter than plain whipped cream, a froth of Chantilly cream is a classic topping. It can be flavored with a few drops of vanilla extract, or a liqueur may be substituted for all or part of the water.

———— **MAKES ABOUT 1 PINT (560 ml)** ————

3 tablespoons water or liqueur
1¼ cups heavy cream, chilled
1 tablespoon sugar
real vanilla extract (optional)

Put the water (or liqueur) into a bowl and chill in the freezer until ice crystals begin to form. Chill the beaters or whisk as well.

Add the cream and whisk until the mixture holds soft peaks. Sprinkle on the sugar and a dash of vanilla, if used, and whisk it in lightly.

Use to decorate ices, coupes or sundaes.

SOFT FRUIT COULIS

Illustrated on pages 56/57

Fresh sauces made with ripe soft fruits complement many ices. Raspberry coulis is the chefs' favorite. Strawberry and mango are also especially good, but any other soft fruit, from peaches to kiwis, can be called upon.
Blackberries, blueberries and black currants all make dramatically dark sauces, and the color and flavor of all three fruits is the better for being lightly cooked. In each case, sweat the fruit in a covered pan over a low heat until the juices begin to run before puréeing it.
I find that I use less and less sugar in fresh fruit sauces — just enough to bring out the best of the flavor. In fact the sugar is here used as a seasoning only

MAKES ABOUT 1 PINT (560 ml)

1 lb ripe raspberries, fresh or frozen and thawed
about 4 tablespoons confectioner's sugar
lemon juice to taste

Purée the raspberries by pressing them through a fine sieve, or by processing them briefly in a blender or food processor then sieving them to remove the seeds.

Stir in the confectioner's sugar and lemon juice to taste, then set the sauce aside for 1 hour, to allow the flavor to develop. Serve chilled.

HOT CHOCOLATE SAUCE

A glossy dark chocolate sauce, that does not harden in contact with ice cream, is an essential addition to every cook's repertoire.

MAKES ABOUT ½ PINT (280 ML)

4 oz (¼ lb) dark chocolate
½ cup corn syrup
2 tablespoons any liqueur (optional)

Break the chocolate into a bowl or the top of a double boiler. Add the syrup or honey and liqueur and stir over simmering water until melted, to make a smooth, hot sauce.

CHOCOLATE FUDGE SAUCE

Condensed milk and plain chocolate make an easy and irresistible hot fudge sauce.

MAKES ABOUT ½ PINT (280 ML)

2 oz (⅛ lb) dark chocolate
½ cup sweetened condensed milk
4 tablespoons fresh milk
1 tablespoon (⅛ stick) unsalted butter

Break the chocolate into a bowl or the top of a double boiler. Add the condensed milk and heat over simmering water, stirring until the chocolate has melted and the sauce is smooth. Beat in the milk, followed by the butter. Serve hot.

CRYSTALIZED FLOWERS
Illustrated on pages 74/75

There is no comparison between the brash color and coarse texture of commercially crystalized flowers – usually violets and roses – and the delicacy of petals frosted at home. It is the simplest of procedures and once done, the flowers will keep for as long as a year.
There are no prettier or more appropriate decorations for ices than fragile, scented, sugared flowers. Not all flowers are edible, of course, but all in the following list are safe: primroses, violets, apple blossom, wallflowers, marigolds, nasturtiums, geraniums, pinks, carnations, roses, jasmine, lilac, borage, orange blossom, and freesias. Check the safety of any flowers not listed.
And all the culinary herbs can be crystalized too, of course.

────────── **50 PETALS OR FLOWERS** ──────────

Fresh, dry flowers in perfect condition – petals or small flowers
1 egg white
1 cup sugar

If you are crystalizing roses, or any other large flowers, separate them into petals. In the case of roses, nip off the white heel at the base of each petal. Very small flowers, individual lilac blossoms, violets and primroses, can be left whole.
Put the egg white into a saucer and break it up a little with a fork.
Spread some of the sugar on a plate and put some more into a small sieve.
Using a small, soft brush, paint each petal or flower lightly all over with egg white. Lay the petals or flowers on the plate of sugar and sprinkle more sugar over them. The sugar sticks best to freshly painted petals, so coat and sugar them one at a time.
Lay the flowers on baking sheets lined with paper and dry them in a barely warm oven or airing cupboard, for 24 hours or until they are dry and brittle. Turn the flowers several times in the first few hours of drying.
The color of the flowers is preserved remarkably well by this method. Once crystalized, flowers should be stored in airtight containers away from bright light.

BASIC SORBET SYRUP

For almost instant ices, basic sorbet syrup is a useful standby. It keeps for several weeks in the refrigerator, ready to combine at a moment's notice with fruit purée or juice and perhaps a liqueur.

────────── **MAKES ABOUT 3 PINTS (1.7 LITRES)** ──────────

1½ lb sugar
1 quart boiling water

Pour the boiling water over the sugar and stir until it has dissolved completely. Cool and store, covered, until needed.

INDEX